SONGS OF A SAGE

ZACHARY D. LYNCH

LONG
OVERDUE

First Edition: December 2025

Title: Songs of a Sage

By: Zachary D. Lynch

Description: First edition.

ISBN 979-8-9939693-1-2

 Formatted with Vellum

For all those in search of the golden mean

CONTENTS

1

A DISTANT REVERIE

A symphony
  A cacophony
  The sounds of a future memory
  The specifics of which I do not know
  Yet had always wanted
  Roused me from a late-night reverie

Thus, I, arising from the fickle bonds of earth
  Fixed my mighty gaze
  My uncertain gaze
  My drowsy gaze
  To the sky
  The stars were dim and unremarkable
  Clouded by village lights
  Yet the very notion of this place
  Intrigued me all the more
  How can it be?
  How can these things be here at once?
  The hissing of nature

The rage of its constituents
>The sheer, untethered state of nature
>Fearlessly beckoning me to return
>To that from which I came
>To leave it in its painful slumber
>Its brutal, unforgiving, unwritten slumber

Yet not so far away
>I can hear it
>The din of a village
>The chaos of civilization
>The devolved, debaucherous croaking
>Of colonists ceaselessly calling me forward
>To that for which they strive
>To forge ahead in blind ambition
>In deaf, mute, thoughtless ambition

In such conflict
>We see who we really are
>Who we are when nobody is watching
>Who we are when everybody is watching
>Who we are when alone with our thoughts

Who am I going to be?
>I, floating through existence like a honeybee
>Seeking flowers and finding them
>And stinging those who interfere
>I, caught in a whirlwind of life
>Like a ship out at sea
>With a home port, a destination,

And turbulent tides
　　I, on the precipice of a story untold
　　Holding a pen yet unsure of what to write

Believing in truth
　　Without knowing its meaning
　　A singer with a song to sing
　　Yet no music to accompany

I seem to get lost every now and then
　　Seem to get in my own way forward
　　Or perhaps my own way backward
　　Stuck in this forever land
　　This temporary land
　　This distant, confusing, never land
　　Who am I going to be?

Will I stay in this tranquility?
　　This confusing, beautiful tranquility?
　　Dangerous and brooding
　　On account of these vicious creatures
　　Eyeing me, licking their chops

Or will I venture forth into the village?
　　Seeking comfort in community
　　Becoming like they are
　　Seeing what truths can result
　　From the destruction of paradise

Forward, I say!
    Forward I must go
    There can be no peace without protection
    There can be no progress without conception
    Though I take comfort in this swamp
    There must be something better
    From our collective effort
    Maybe I will find I am like them after all?

Surely, something good will come from
    All that blaring and blasting
    Whims and whispering
    Clatter and chattering
    Hoping and praying
    Cannot be for naught
    Even a rose may bloom amid such thorns

Striding onward
    Possessing nothing
    Remembering nothing
    Dreaming of everything
    I journeyed toward those bright, gaudy lights
    That separate us from our birthright

Yes, onward I strode.

2

THE BALLAD OF TINSEL
AND CELLOPHANE

After much striding
　　Much venturing into that great unknown
　　I, at long last, found myself entering the village
　　Shining bright like tinsel
　　A contrived glow in this innate unknown
　　Sprouting up from the soil
　　As if it had been put there by a Higher Power
　　But no
　　Nothing like this
　　Could ever be wrought by omniscience

Neither divine architect above
　　Nor mortal fountainhead below
　　Could have envisioned this
　　Only a falling morning star
　　Only a clipping of angel's wings
　　Could have willed this form of creation
　　Could have inspired its sprouting from these lands
　　Still wet from yesterday's dewfall

And, oh, the scenes I saw!
    The visions I had!
    Unlike anything from my wildest imagination
    The people wandered about
    Loveless
    Thoughtless
    Faithless
    Ignorant
    Baking in the hot sun
    Yet irked by the darkness of their own shadows

Shackled by chains, they were
    Chains they, themselves, had mindlessly wrapped
    Around their twisted, depraved bodies
    Like a bird meant to soar through the clouds
    Yet trapped in a cage of its own creation
    Indeed, both hold the key to their own salvation
    To their future
    If only they were brave enough
    Wise enough to use it

No community I found in this village of individuals
    With their eyes down toward the earth
    Instead of turning left and right
    To investigate the state of their existence
    Or turning up to pierce the heavens
    To see the machinations
    The cogs and springs and mechanisms
    That lay beyond

Nay they had done away with all of that
    The hopes of which had brought me to this village
    They could not see the violence in their streets
    Or in their hearts
    They could not see the filth in their rivers
    Or in their souls
    They could not see the harm of their actions
    Or of their omissions
    So absorbed were they
    In the strange, mangled paths
    Of the cracks in the sidewalks
    Predicting the twists and turns
    Rather than healing them

Content with a chuckle
    Instead of a bellow
    Content to whisper
    Rather than sing
    Content to sit
    As if they had forgotten how to dance
    Content to flail their arms in an inner sanctum
    To repose in a surly chamber,
    Closed off from the world
    Content to take only a sip
    From a chalice they had inherited
    And which held enough to quench a thirst
    To which they had long been accustomed

No one paid me any mind
    I drifted about unnoticed
    Unheard

Unseen
    In that sense, I was one and the same
    With the people
    Who had traded all the world
    For an assortment of clay and mud
    Mixed with cellophane
    And who had traded virtue
    For a pocketful of marbles
    And an afternoon of revelry

Though pretty it was
    It surely could not shine a light
    To the dreams of the driver of the first nail
    The layer of the first brick
    On this tenuous and flat soil

I wondered aloud if I would have been better off
    Staying in that distant swamp
    Among creatures harmonious with nature
    Incapable of striving for more
    Yet living out their fullest potential
    Yes, I wondered aloud
    "Who am I going to be?"

And then, as if on cue
    I heard the shrill cry of a Sage
    Seated upon a street corner in the center of town
    "At last," said he,
    As he arose from the concrete

"The time has come for us to pick up the lantern
    Thrown down all those years ago
    The morning hours are gone
    And now the sun shines brightly!
    How brightly it shines in the heat of the day!
    The sponge is among us
    Can't you see it?
    It still contains the ink of an old horizon
    Wiped away blindly and unwillingly
    By the charred and gnarled hands of our forefathers

Far too long have we gone without a horizon
    Drifting aimlessly through space and time
    Betrothed neither to what lies above nor below
    The time for a tremendous event is now!
    The crack of lightning
    The bolt of thunder
    Have now reached the shores of this swamp
    This first frontier among ever-rising tides

Hear me if you will
    And hear me true
    For I will try to show this place
    To the light of the stars
    They may look hazy with these lights
    But they are still shining brightly
    Yes, like a million little lanterns in the sky
    If only you'd be willing to bear the pain of seeing them
    A momentary pang
    Like the brightness of exiting the only cave
    You had ever known

Yes, you could regain your focus
 And return to your nature
 Like a droplet of water flying through the air
 Momentarily airborne, the force of a rock in a riverbed
 Returning at last to whitewater rapids
 Flowing steadily forward
 Yes, ever forward."

The people looked at him for a brief moment
 One brief shining moment
 But, unconvinced, they
 Returned to the banality
 Of the ever-deepening sidewalk cracks

Sensing this, the Sage continued
 "Perhaps not enough time has gone by
 Perhaps this message has again arrived too soon
 Perhaps the embers of the old lantern still shine
 And have not gone cold with the winds of time
 But this I cannot accept
 I cannot wait on nature
 To will this moment into existence
 To take agency over these disenfranchised
 If you with ears will not turn them to me
 I will give you a reason to."

Grimacing slightly, the Sage held up a box and exclaimed
 "I have here a $50 Amazin' gift card
 Turn me your ear for a moment
 And you, too, can get two-day free shipping."

Then the people looked up from the sidewalk cracks
    Fixed their gaze upon the Sage
    And slowly
    Gradually
    Meandered over to him

Indeed, deliverance must know its audience
    Or risk being ignored
    And forgotten
    Like the bones of a structure
    That once housed a family
    And knew joy
    Yet now lies in ruinous rapture
    On the outskirts of memory

I, hearing all this
    Whether to see the light of the stars
    Or for the promise of two-day free shipping
    Also meandered over to the Sage
    Took my perch near the street corner
    Among the masses
    As he began to speak

3

A SONG OF HAPPINESS

Addressing the burgeoning crowd
>   Hungry for the promise of gift cards
>   The Sage spoke

"I look upon you all
>   And see nothing but a void
>   Yes, staring out at you
>   I see nothing but an abyss in return
>   I bear witness
>   That this abyss is too dark for me
>   Where is the light of your life?

You, who do not know why you were put on this soil
>   Who know not your purpose in life
>   Must know that happiness is neither detractor
>   Nor distraction
>   And only knows how to bring light

Remember this
    You, who spend your days toiling away
    In service of the gargantuan
    And of the minute
    Of things you admire
    And of things you despise
    Of things you believe in
    And of things you do not
    Of things which command you to remember
    And of things which compel you to forget
    Of legacies and notoriety
    And of trials and tribulations
    And everything in between
    Should make happiness a priority

Where there is good food
    Eat well
    Where there is good company
    Laugh loudly
    Where there is festivity
    Be merry
    Where there is revelry
    Give song
    Where there is need for a lighthouse in a storm
    Shine brightly
    And where the quietness of the heart summons
    Be still and listen

Hear this now
    That happiness begins by deriving joy from this
    The passage of time

And the constant that is change
    Through stupor and splendor
    Through hell and high water
    From the depths of a valley,
    Examining the majestic mountain
    From its peak, gazing out at the rugged expanse below
    Yes, through the dark of night
    When illuminated only by the light of the moon
    Remember: the darkest moment occurs
    Just before the break of dawn
    That a ball thrown from up high
    Bounces upward again only upon hitting rock bottom
    That when you are tired from the whirlwind of life
    It will not be long before you catch your breath
    And that when the situation appears most dire
    You can confidently say 'it can only get better
    For this cannot last forever.'

Remember this,
    And govern yourself accordingly
    Be like the breaking of the dawn
    As if guaranteed by nature
    Be like a ball bouncing
    In unquestioning unity with physical law
    Give breath to those who need it
    And in this breath bestow kindness
    To the despairing masses
    For, like all things, such struggles cannot last forever
    But a bit of respite is a welcome refuge
    To those caught in the headwinds of existence

Therein, I say, lies happiness
    In enjoying the passage of time
    And making it better for others
    This precious process is what makes us human
    Distinguishes us from other creatures in this swamp
    So as you go about your business
    Remember not to dwell on tomorrow's uncertainties
    At the expense of the light of today

My words, like all things
    Shall pass through the sands of time
    And be carried by the wind to their eternal rest
    In the interim, let them not fall on ears
    Deafened by the darkness of this abyss before me

Amen, I say to you
    While you can and while you may
    Be happy."

4

A SONG OF HEALTH

"But wait,"
 Cried one from the crowd
 "If everything is temporary
 Then what of our health?
 What of all these miles I walk
 What of all these quantified burdens I carry?
 What of my measured portions
 And carefully constructed routine?"

"Know this,"
 Said the Sage
 "Health is no binary thing
 It is neither positive nor negative
 It is neither a yes nor a no

It is rather a pendulum constantly in motion
 A spectrum on which we all find ourselves
 And on which there is nothing to cling

Who among us can claim perfect health
    In such a state of bliss?

Strengthen yourself
    Improve your body
    This is important
    For your body is a vehicle,
    It must be driven every day
    A chariot that moves in one direction only
    Cannot be insured against the caprices of this world
    Or the procrastination of your mind's darkest corner

Amen, I say to you
    As you break down your body
    And your mind
    You build it back better than before
    As you break down your limitations
    You reconstruct a soul greater than before
    As you break down your tolerance for the comfort
    Of a soft armchair and a black coffee in the early morn
    Or a worn sofa and a red wine in the early evening
    You forge for yourself a new state of being
    Which carries you forward
    High above this fleeting, floating universe

This world
    This ongoing ballad of tinsel and cellophane
    Late to rise and late to slumber
    Inoculated by a bit of poison
    Resting in unenlightened ecstasy upon a fairy's wing

Lives freely and momentarily
 And will soon meet the common due
 Unwilling and unprepared
 Yes, you who have strengthened yourself
 Will be better prepared
 But will not be fully insulated
 From the gyrations of the cosmos

Because hear me this!
 No one will remember the gasps you heaved
 No one will remember the load you carried
 As you struggled mightily against the asymptotes
 Imposed by that which brought you out of the swamp
 From which you came
 Though you may be filled with pride and satisfaction
 That the world appears to have been set aflame
 You must remember this alone is not important
 And will be like the dewfall
 Evaporated by the first sheen of the morning light

For health is a juggling act
 In which we all must find balance
 Between the journey and destination
 Between the means and the ends
 Otherwise you will be like a gleaming galleon
 Glimmering before a setting sun
 Never again to see its home port

Yes, too much poison and lethargy
 Can wreak havoc on the body and soul

And lay rust upon a beautiful machine
    Meant for so much more
    But in small doses will help us
    Drift off to sleep
    Encourage the passage of time
    Inhibit inhibitions
    And will add contour
    To the winding, weaving cracks in the sidewalk

While poison and revelry
    Will never furnish a canvas
    It may on occasion inspire us to pick up our palettes
    As we were meant to do
    And add color to the story of our lives
    Add context to our venture out of the swamp
    And make our juggling act
    The rising and falling of discrete portions of our lives
    Through the thickened air
    A florid display of our most profound selves
    This, too, is important

For one cannot fly high
    Without having wings strong enough
    To elevate oneself upward
    And carry on through the cold of a lonely night
    But so, too, is it that one cannot fly for long,
    At so great a height
    And above a universe this large
    Without having a spirit to persevere
    And without a home to which to return

Yes, I beseech you
    Do not be like Narcissus, silently spinning
    Smiling only at the sight of yourself, alone,
    Failing to admire the magnificence around
    Above and below

Yes, I beseech you
    Do not be like Icarus, soaring to great heights
    Inching closer to the lofty and divine
    While forgetting what exists down below
    For though you may be beautiful
    And, yes, you are beautiful!
    You will never truly see the beauty you manifest
    If you fail to remember that
    It is both internal and external
    Within and without."

5

A SONG OF COGNIZANCE

By this time,
    The Sage's words had caused quite a commotion
    And others, having heard
    Began wandering over
    Attracted by neither truth nor two-day shipping
    But rather by curiosity
    Not by a desire to know
    But by a desire to be in the know
    Not out of a fear of ignorance
    But rather out of a fear of missing out

Just then shouted another from the crowd
    In red, hot anger
    "Who are you, with these fancy words?
    Who anointed you king of this street corner?
    Who gave you the power to speak to us all
    As if by divine decree?
    You have caused enough of a ruckus
    And are blocking our path!

Quit your perch
    And let us go about our business in peace!"

To this, the Sage calmly replied
    "Friends, remember always
    To hear *what* others speak
    And not *how* they speak
    Remember always to feast on substance
    And not on style
    Blessed are those who pick the diamond in the rough
    For theirs is the light of truth and compassion
    While others is to fester alone in splitting silence

Indeed, if there is one thing which you hear today
    Let it be a call to look up from the sidewalk cracks
    Obsess not on the fractures of your path
    Predict no more their twists and turns
    Wager not on the paths of ants who run in their gullies
    And get washed away by the rainfall

Instead look up and look around
    For the whole of creation is before your very eyes!
    Can't you see the blue sky
    In between these buildings so high?
    Can't you see the trees bearing sweet fruit
    While nourished by concrete?
    Can't you see a Higher Power
    In stained glass
    Or leaves of grass?
    Who among us has not enjoyed

The fruits of the labor of others?
    Have you not stopped a moment
    To ponder the grandeur
    Of how the nectar you sip
    Went from a distant land
    To dismal lips?
    You with eyes to see
    Can't you see the brilliance
    Of this harmonious dichotomy?

Never before has there been such an opportunity
    With the acrylic panes in your pockets
    For uninhibited pursuit of the human and the divine
    With the power to illuminate the world
    You choose to magnify
    Only the sidewalk cracks before you
    When this is bound to hurt your eyes
    Poison your mind
    And cause you to tumble
    Toward gullies illuminated
    By such unnatural light

You were made to look for windows
    Yet settle for mirrors
    You were made to climb atop mountains
    And swim across seas
    Yet anger yourself when your path is blocked
    By such trifles as this
    Indeed, ingenuity has handed you a gift horse
    And you, blinded by acrylic light,
    Have looked it in the mouth

When led to the banks of the river
    Dive in and open up your heart
    When led to fields of green
    Fall in and open up your soul
    When surrounded by that which makes you wonder
    Look around and open your mind
    When entrusted with acrylic light
    Do not cast it to the gullies
    Or to your own eyes
    When you can turn its brightness up to the sky

Amen, I say to you
    Do not dispense with the world at your feet
    For the world at your fingertips
    For much can be learned
    Beyond that which fits in the palm of your hand
    Or which sits idly
    In the recesses of your consciousness."

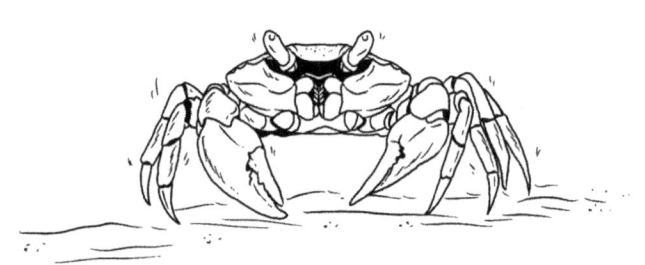

6

THE FIRST INTERMISSION

"Wait a moment!"
 Shouted a man from the crowd
 "I am engaged in industry in this village
 And know you are doing a disservice
 To those who lent you their ears
 You who encourage us to give song
 Should allow me the chance
 To opine on a matter of great importance."

"Speak, friend!"
 Said the Sage
 Beckoning with an extended arm
 The man toward the street corner
 "Let your truth be known to us
 Come forth! And share the song of your soul."

A young woman next to the man
 Turned to him, wide-eyed and exasperated

Shaking her head and tugging his arm
    Begging him to stay by her side
    And not join the Sage
    But I saw him brush her off
    Dismiss her concerns
    Like a child with a candy wrapper
    As he rose from the masses
    Becoming one with the heat waves
    Levitating from their cobblestone perch
    Emanating toward the street corner

Making way for the man's arrival
    The Sage ceded a portion of the street corner
    With a smile on his face
    Eager to see flowers bloom in a concrete garden
    Hungry to let pass the lips of this village
    The nectar of their new fruits
    Born and bred by the songs of the sage
    And nourished between the sidewalk cracks
    Perhaps the time is nigh after all?

The man, having now arrived at the street corner
    Looked out at the ever-widening crowd
    His nervous eyes met my own for a brief moment
    And related to me in unspoken word
    That he faced the same daunting question
    The same haunting, age-old question
    "Who am I going to be?"
    Overcoming timidity, the man took a deep breath
    And spoke unto the crowd

"Songs of a Sage would not be possible
    Without viewers and listeners like you
    And the generous support of our sponsors
    Like Autovana
    With Autovana, you can get pre-qualified
    On the used car of your dreams
    From their easy-to-use mobile app!
    They offer all makes and models
    With favorable financing terms
    And over a million AI-generated videos
    So that you can know exactly what you're buying
    Before you buy it!
    Autovana is embracing cutting-edge AI technology
    To ensure that you can always
    GET THE CAR SIGHT UNSEEN
    For a limited time, use the code SAGE7 in the app
    To obtain 7% APR upon approval
    Again, that's all-caps S-A-G-E and then the number 7
    Other restrictions may apply."

Incredulously, the Sage looked upon the man
    "Favorable though those terms may be
    Surely that is not what brought you
    Upon this street corner
    Your wit and wisdom
    Must have been nurtured
    By more everlasting things."

Without verbal response
    The man thus extended his arm toward the Sage
    Or rather, toward the box of Amazin' gift cards

Fingers desperate for two-day free shipping
  Only to find that the Sage
  Summarily moved the box out of his range
  Eliminating, at least for a moment
  Its alluring promise

In a vain attempt to reason with the Sage
  The man uttered unto him
  "Come on, let me get one of those
  I just helped you out here
  Do you have a TikTok?
  You'd definitely go viral."
  Replied the Sage
  With neither anger nor resentment on his face
  "The time is not yet nigh
  But, alas, is growing closer
  Friend, I can see it clearly
  The woman you accompanied here
  Has grown embarrassed by your presence
  Quit this street corner
  And return to her
  For you still have much to learn."

Clicking his tongue in frustration
  The man turned his back toward the Sage
  And migrated back to the multitude
  Who parted before him like supple trees
  Before hurricane-force winds
  Or, perhaps, it was the Sage
  From the street corner
  Who parted the multitude

Like an elder Sage had once parted the Red Sea
    Alas, I could not tell

However, before entering
    The man shouted out once more to the crowd
    "Additional support for Songs of a Sage
    Was provided by DividedHealthcare
    'There for what matters to us'
    Speak to your human resources department
    About switching to a DividedHealthcare plan
    Or ask me about supplemental or gap coverage
    I'll be handing out business cards after the program."

The man took his position next to the young woman
    Whose eyes, as the Sage had noted
    Were wide and bright white
    In contrast to the redness of her cheeks
    And staring down at the cobblestones beneath her
    Avoiding the scorn and ridicule of the multitude
    But it seemed to me
    That no one was paying her any mind
    Whence, then, came her embarrassment?
    From her fear of their perceived judgment?
    From her understanding of the melody
    Undergirding the Sage's song?
    Alas, I could not tell

Thus spoke the Sage
    "Dear friends, I come not with sponsorship
    For truth cannot sprout forth from the root of all evil

I engage with neither metal dealer nor money lender
    Nor middleman nor parasite
    I speak only the song of the universe
    Which calls unto you and to me
    And allows you to dwell in comfort in your quarter
    Without demanding any pieces of silver
    Amen, I say to you
    No amalgamation destined to rust in oblivion
    No unturned table in this village
    No ransom paid to a hostage-taker
    No crab scuttling across the floors of treacherous seas
    Is worth even a penny of your existence

Hear me true, dear friends
    From the swamp they came
    And to the swamp they shall return!
    Be not beguiled by their charms
    For there is more to life than such chicanery
    Indeed, there is a greater truth within
    Unable to be expressed
    In a soundbite purchased by the highest bidder."

7

A SONG OF SPIRITUALITY

"Sage, what more is there to life?"
Asked another from the still increasing crowd
"I believe there is more to life than
That which we see and feel
I believe in the light of what is to come
And have heard the promise of its virtue
Oh, how we would appreciate the indulgence
Of your speaking to us about spirituality."

Spoke the Sage
"You who seek ultimate solace
Will find none here
You who long for wisdom
To hold your hand and whisper in your ear
Will encounter nothing of the sort
You who wander the earth
Endeavoring to draw lines
Connecting the stars above
Will conclude your sojourn

Lightheaded and heavyhearted
 And in the same place in which you began
 For such deeper truths do not appear
 From reason alone

For all you who have received the gift of faith
 And all you who have not
 Must know there is light on this earth
 Yes, indeed there is light on this earth!
 There is balm in Gilead!
 Can't you smell its pungent fumes
 As they seep through this village
 Arcing downward from the sky
 And swinging up from the earth
 Through the very cobblestones on which we stand?

A fish may know nothing of the meadow
 But it surely knows the feeling of water on its gills
 A land animal may know nothing of the seabed
 But it must know the feeling of the wind in its face
 Amen I say to you
 We know nothing of the divine
 But we must know the sound
 Of its revelation here on earth

It is not a loud sound
 But rather faint and dim
 With a symphonic tone
 Surely you can hear it too
 Echoing from the condemned at Calvary

Pouring outward from the flames on Horeb
    Sounding from the mountaintop at Arafat
    Or perhaps from an even deeper truth within
    The sounds are growing fainter
    After so many years
    But they can still be heard
    If only you with ears to hear
    Will lend them to the earth

Let me speak what I have heard
    And it is only what I have heard with human ears
    I am not the Messiah
    I am not a prophet
    I go about life unburdened
    By the weight of the infinite
    And knowing it will all end

I come to you as one of you
    And only of you
    Born from this earth
    Condemned to die on this earth
    Dust to dust
    Light to light
    And this is enough
    For my own reason
    Matched with revelation
    Is enough to hear the song of the earth
    And enough to grant me peace
    And so should it with you

Who among us knows with certainty
    What is to come next?
    Who among us would trade a bird in the hand
    For two in the bush?
    Who among us has such faith
    In transliterations of transliterations
    Passed from tongue to tongue
    And tide to tide
    To these weaving, winding streets
    That he or she turns a blind eye
    To the beauty of that which lays before us
    And will come to lay before us?
    My dear friends
    This is not faith
    This is hope runneth over
    This is blindly following
    That which was handed down to you
    In unquestioning, unremitting loyalty

Hear me true
    As I recount the sounds I hear
    As they ripple softly across the land
    And shake the heavens!

Remember that there is more than this earth
    Yes, there is a Higher Power
    But we cannot know about any Higher Power
    Except that which is revealed to us
    And that such revelation cannot be sought
    Or bought
    But read in a script

For a play in which we are cast
    But do not direct

Remember that this Higher Power knows no province
    And has no favored people
    So be neither pious nor pompous
    Neither gaudy nor grandstanding
    Take your steps in service to others
    In love for the earth
    Rather than in service of yourself
    For though the earth may be cold and challenging
    It and its inhabitants are a blessing
    It is worth its weight
    And is worth its struggle

Remember that this Higher Power knows no creed
    And does not speak one tongue alone
    But instead reveals Itself in many ways
    Without having a name by which to call Itself
    Accordingly be critical and free in your thoughts
    Remain skeptical
    And be not bound by dogma or doctrine
    For there is no telling where or when
    Such revelation will occur next

Remember also that this Higher Power
    Seeks neither to convert nor compel
    But rather to inspire and impassion
    Be not so certain in your beliefs
    That you are blind to your realities

For that is not in accordance with nature
    And will only incur disfavor

Remember to live a good life for its own sake
    And not for the sake of the indefinite
    For it is better to approach life with reason
    And be reasonable in your approach to life
    For this is the secret to salvation
    Do not depart this earth
    For what is to come
    Without having truly experienced
    What it means to live
    For death is not a worse fate than this

Amen I say to you
    This is what is revealed to all
    By the music of the earth
    Listen closely
    And listen true
    And do not let these dulcet tones
    Softly pass you by
    Into the ethos."

8

A SONG OF LOVE

"But how are we to love the earth
    And others and ourselves?"
    Quipped one from the crowd
    "What does it mean to love?"

Spoke the Sage
    "You, who are encircling me
    Keep one eye on these Amazin' gift cards
    Which brought you here
    But this is not in accordance with nature!
    You point and choose
    And the sum total of human ingenuity
    Arrives on your doorsteps in two days
    You aim and click
    And all the world can appear
    In instant gratification
    But this is not how real love works

Love is the blood in your veins
    And the beating of your heart
    The spark of a match
    And the lighting of a candle in the dark
    The spinning of the earth
    And the sunrise on a warm summer day
    It is both giving and taking
    A waltz and a score
    With both major and minor chords
    It is the donation of a part of your soul
    With the hope that it be received warmly
    Or returned rather than disposed
    Though love has many faces
    Its smile is one and the same

But before you can see any of these faces
    You must first know and appreciate yourself
    You must love yourself
    Warts, carbuncles, aching backs, aching souls
    Yes, before all else
    Before you can participate in the lives of others
    Or enhance your own
    You must accept yourself as you are
    Flawed and fragile
    Stagnate or conflagrate
    Progressing or retrogressing
    You must come as you are!
    For true love in all its forms
    Requires space and separation
    Which can only be achieved
    When you are at peace with yourself

There is love for your family
    An innate kinship unbroken by time or space
    This unconditional love is a blessing
    But even for those who know not such blessings
    Or perhaps know them with conditions
    Must know that blood is thicker than water
    And that even when it stings
    Such love makes you more resilient
    And more open to its other forms
    Which is a blessing in disguise

Those who reared you know you best
    And have seen you as no one else has
    Their love is the purest
    And its truest form
    Its most aspirational form
    The hub upon which all spokes depend
    The stars upon which all else is oriented
    And the force which guides our nature
    Just as gravity guides a falling feather
    Down to restful repose
    Amen, I say to you
    All love derives from this

There is also love for your friends
    The family you have chosen
    Although blood may be thicker than water
    Water is necessary to quench your thirst
    Such love adds color to our souls
    And contrast to our shadows
    And without which we would wither

Like a plant in the desert sun
    Pursue your friends with vigor
    And they shall embrace you
    As you embrace yourself

But be not beguiled
    By the viscosity of false friends
    Those only interested in the fleeting
    And in the temporary
    Those only interested in sitting on the shore
    Of your personhood
    Rather than diving in
    And riding the waves of your life
    While this may satisfy you in the short term
    You will find that their quench
    Meets your tongue like sea water
    While you lay adrift in the ocean
    As these friends come and go from your view
    Do not crane your head or stretch your arms
    In a vain effort to keep them within reach
    For sometimes the bravest thing
    The most difficult thing
    The correct thing
    Is to let go

Remember also
    That there is love for the world
    For the strangers in your midst
    And, yes, even for the sidewalk cracks
    As you navigate these cobblestones
    As a great Sage once said

'Be curious, not judgmental.'
    Shine a light on a stranger's day
    And bring a smile
    Just as real love can do for you

But I would be remiss
    If I did not touch upon love for another
    Wrought from your most mortal sentiment
    Which burns passionately like a fire
    On a cold winter's night
    Although the flames of this fire shine brightly
    And radiate heat across your body
    Remember that this love is not a union of flesh
    But a union of souls
    Live sensually and in the moment
    But do not prioritize the temporal over the everlasting

While you may be tempted to pursue such flames
    As often as they come along
    To launch yourself blind and willingly
    Into sweet and tender warmth
    The smile will evaporate from your face
    As you watch your flesh scale and wither around you
    Leaving you charred and skinless
    And your subcutaneous self exposed for all the world
    In this moment, you will crave warmth from another
    But find each touch feeling like salt in an open wound

Dear friends, love is not the night sky
    But rather an illuminating shooting star

Love is not monochrome
>   But rather a kaleidoscope
>   Love is a bright red rose
>   With beautiful petals and sharp thorns
>   Which you are meant to hold up as your own
>   Like a lantern for all the world to see
>   With blood dripping down your wrist
>   Uniting the rose's hue with your flesh
>   As your love has done for you

Do not resolve yourselves for anything less
>   And do not be blind to the fact
>   That in any of love's faces
>   Power does not rest equally
>   But rather vests exclusively
>   And ironically
>   In the person for whom it is less important
>   Know that while this may cause pain
>   From time to time, such pain is momentary
>   And like all things
>   Shall soon pass like a breath expelled
>   Condensed as a white fog
>   Into the crisp night air
>   As the others in your life
>   Your other cherished and beloved
>   Wait inside with lights and hot tea
>   With gauze and a soothing balm
>   Until such time as you find in another
>   Enough comfort and separation
>   That the flames do not break you down
>   But rather build you up, as one soul in two bodies
>   Forevermore

Yes indeed
　　Love is scarring and scary
　　Kind and consoling
　　Painful and potent
　　Ubiquitous and unbound
　　And worth every while
　　But hear me true!
　　There is no love for the inanimate
　　Your Amazin' accounts will come and go
　　In momentary glory
　　And leave you forever wanting more
　　Instead, real love is not being-in
　　But being-for

Amen I say to you
　　Love is the alpha and omega
　　The beginning and the end
　　Hold it closely always
　　And cherish it accordingly
　　Let it dwell among you
　　And take refuge in your home
　　Let it permeate your lexicon
　　And give voice to your soul
　　Though it burns like a fire
　　Fear not the striking of the match

Do this and you, too, shall know true joy
　　True existence."

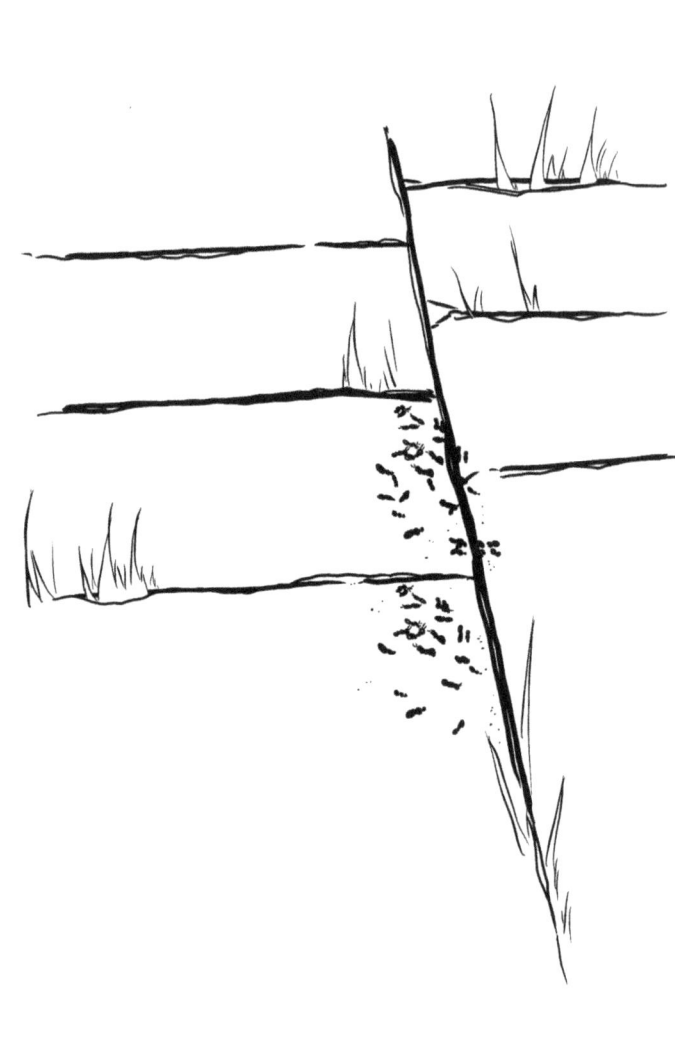

9

A SONG OF MINDFULNESS

"Who am I going to be?"
   I wondered aloud again
   As the din of the crowd grew larger
   Made uneasy by the Sage and his words
   Challenging the essence of this village
   Of its inhabitants
   And its sidewalk cracks

I noticed the arrival of police officers
   Heads bowed and ears turned
   To a beady-eyed member of the crowd
   Eyes fierce and fists gnarled
   Shaking angrily in the direction of the Sage
   Apparently communicating his rage
   At the contents of the Sage's message
   What was so distressing, I wondered,
   That would merit such earthly intervention?
   Perhaps the Sage was right
   That the embers of the old lantern

Thrown down years ago in desperation
    Still burned bright enough to blind the eyes
    Of the village inhabitants

Sensing this, the Sage spoke again
    "Dear friends,
    Have my words offended you?
    Have I caused you harm?
    I come with a message of joy and peace
    My aim is only to speak truth
    Do you not see that this is why I came here
    That this is why I am among you?
    Surely you know that all of us have a task to do
    Teachers, dreamers, doers
    Of all stripes and styles
    And yes, this includes the police
    Who are now surrounding our group
    Theirs is to ensure the civility of this village
    To protect law and order
    This is a noble calling
    But how, pray tell,
    Has this street corner
    Returned to the state of nature?

Is it possible the lines have been crossed?
    Do we still desire that which we cannot hold?
    Has the turmoil ordinarily confined
    To a microscope's lens
    Suddenly been put on display
    For all the world to see?

Has the light in your eyes gone dark
> After so many years without a dream to dream?
> Have your souls fallen silent
> After so many years without a song to sing?
> Perhaps, indeed, the time for a tremendous event
> Is not yet nigh?
> Perhaps it will only come
> Once the incarnation is complete
> Once the sun has dried up the sea
> Uniting at long last
> A rising and setting sun
> With the underbelly of that which
> We hide beneath the sea?

Perhaps you are too drawn to the sidewalk cracks
> That my words have fallen short!
> After all it is true
> That the grandest ruse the Devil ever pulled
> Was convincing people he did not walk among us
> While the greatest malady in communication
> Is the illusion that it has transpired
> And so, my dear friends,
> While I have this moment
> Allow me to clarify my message
> And to apply it to the nature of work
> As appears to me in this village
> For this applies not only to my task
> But also to yours

I beseech you all
> Fix your eyes once again on the sidewalk cracks

Which beckon you so earnestly
    And you will see ants and spiders and other insects
    Digging intricate tunnels and spinning intricate webs
    You will see weeds and crabgrass
    Sprouting forth and letting their presence be known
    Now, as I have shown you to do
    Look above you
    And you will see birds soaring high
    Building nests and surveying all the lands
    Now, as your forefathers had before
    Look out at the swamp from which you came
    To see its creatures writhing and wriggling
    As if to a tune only they can hear
    But who among us can disagree
    That all this is in accordance with nature?

Now, dear friends, I beseech you again
    Look to your left and right
    Tell me true, what do you see?
    Do you have the courage to say what you see?
    As it is and not as you would wish it to be?
    Are you living in accordance with nature?
    Or have you become untethered
    Floating quietly, aimlessly
    Throughout our speck of existence?
    You who are late to rise and late to slumber
    Slaving away your days
    In ceaseless repetition
    And hopeless ambition
    Are you doing what you were made to do?
    If you were posed with that ultimate question
    'Could you tell me why?'

Which makes martyrs and kings
    You would be still as catatonic
    Still stuck in the abyss
    Which renders before me
    Unchanged and uninhibited
    Your sad and stolid state

In this realm
    The echoes of the Higher Power do not reverberate
    Instead reason shall guide us forth
    As I join with the birds
    And sing for you the song of my soul
    Rather than of the creation
    Dear friends, hear me true
    We were not made to sit upon the mountainside
    And imagine the view from above
    We are not meant to lie beside the railroad tracks
    And wonder where the whistles stop
    We were not made to pass through life in misery
    Endlessly banging a hammer
    Against an unsinkable nail
    While running through the green fields of our minds
    Amen I say to you
    Our lot is not to pursue such fickle things

You were made to rise in the morning
    With joie de vivre
    Ready to set forth into the day
    Like a fish to water
    For this you must fill your hours
    With tasks that fill your mind and soul

So that you may perform them fully
    And fix your aim toward that for which
    You would part ways with your own life
    Amen, I say to you
    The meaning of life is death!
    The light of day means nothing without the night
    Your heart's desire is nothing without its craving
    Joy means nothing without sorrow

Your dedication to anything less than death
    Is a lifelong commitment to an interim of
    Vacillation and vicissitude
    As you were born on this earth
    So, too, are you condemned to die on this earth!
    You will make like a sunflower
    Shining brightly and beautifully
    Before turning your gaze to the wilting horizon
    Meeting death like an old friend
    Dear friends, this is not brutish but benign
    By design to add perspective to our days

You who have been granted the gift of mindfulness
    Not bestowed on any other creature in the swamp
    Opt to trade it for tasks that fail to fulfill you
    Your days drag by, your years yearn for more
    You choose to squander yourself
    On false prophets with plastic altars
    On acrylic light and gold-plated teaspoons
    Though these shine brightly in the moment
    They erode with the sands of time

Leaving your birthright a chipped and unsightly mess
    And you all the worse for it

Amen, I say to you
    Seek tasks that bring you joy and fulfillment
    Seek tasks that speak to your soul and its talents
    Seek tasks that leave the earth in a better place
    Than the earth you received
    These three, my dear friends
    Allow you to unlock your greatest gift
    Gold and silver will fill your dwellings
    And your bellies
    But starve your souls
    I beseech you again
    Waste not a moment more in pursuit of anything less
    Than your death's deepest desire

But you think I speak only of work?
    Be not so simplistic
    This may hand you a pen and paper
    But the task of writing remains outstanding
    Unbridled pursuit of your death's desire
    Gives you the energy to rise
    Out of bed and to the sky
    Yes, you will rise!
    But you must be temperate in your rise
    As in all things
    Both to yourself and to others around you
    For your laborious self is not your whole self
    But merely one part of a grander vision
    One thread in the tapestry of your life

One stroke upon the canvas
    Which adorns the easel of your existence

Hear me true!
    Be not so absorbed in your tasks
    As you are in the sidewalk cracks
    That it is to the detriment of your other selves
    For so it is that labor may amplify your voice
    But it will not give you a song to sing
    Industry may provide a platform
    But it will not give you a sweeping view to see
    Your tasks may bestow you with stars
    But no sky upon which to hang them
    Amen, I say to you
    Your achievements fulfill one area of life
    But enjoyment thereof will only come from equipoise
    From temperance and moderation
    The ultimate pursuit of virtue
    Leading to equilibrium among all your selves

Your labor and your rise
    May grant you a position of authority
    Which may be wielded among others
    But you, too, should heed me this
    Let not your thirst for influence satiate your senses,
    Be not so drunk on power
    That you stumble to great heights
    Be not so blind in ambition
    That you fail to see the horizon
    The perfectly pristine partition
    Which separates us from what lies above and below

Let your gravitas be an acceptance of a vocation
    And let your acceptance, too, be gentle and temperate
    For in those to whom much has been given
    Much is ever expected
    In those to whom trust has been endowed
    Kindness and generosity is demanded
    In those who have been charged
    With managing the affairs of others
    Treat it as an opportunity to improve the world
    No matter how great or small its magnitude
    And refrain from its abuse

With this in mind, dear friends,
    You, too, can inherit the world
    And leave it a better place
    For the prosperity of our posterity."

10

THE SECOND INTERMISSION

Suddenly, there came another voice from the crowd
    "Oh, Sage!"
    Cried a young woman
    Yes, mine eyes fail me not
    It was the same young woman whose sheepish gaze
    Graced the cobblestones in fabricated shame
    When not so long ago
    The man by her side graced the street corner
    Spoke the young woman
    "Sensing your great wisdom
    I would cherish the chance
    To ask you a question
    Which, no doubt, many of us have."

"What troubles you, friend?"
    Inquired the Sage
    Turning his gaze and taking slight steps
    Weighted with authority toward her

"Lacking wisdom, myself
    I cannot offer it to you
    But I will endeavor to answer you
    As best I can in accordance with nature
    Step forward and be heard."

This time, it fell upon the man to her side
    To look upon her with bewilderment
    To reach for her arm as if to pull her back
    Into the warm embrace of the crowd
    But, alas, to no avail
    Quelling trepidation
    The young woman had already stepped into the open
    With the crowd parted, just as before,
    And thus planting her feet firmly
    Between the cobblestones
    She spoke unto the Sage

"Do you have a podcast?
    If you don't, you totally should make one
    I can make you famous far beyond this village
    'The Sage Experience' would be such a good name
    Or maybe 'Call Him Sage'
    I don't know, we could figure it out later
    You could have guests on your podcast
    And talk to them about your message
    It's so edgy and retro
    You could get paid in more than just gift cards
    And could reach people all over the world
    It would be so en vogue. What do you think?"

Upon hearing this, the crowd erupted in applause
    The loudest reaction yet

From a group which heretofore
    Had largely stared in silence
    The Sage, somewhat startled by this reaction
    Raised his hands to calm the crowd
    Catching the loud vibrations thundering his way
    Absorbing them with poise
    And returning only sheer tranquility
    After a short while, the crowd had thus calmed
    And with an ever gentle voice
    The Sage continued

"You seek to make a spectacle of me
    Indeed, you see dripping from my mouth
    Gold and frankincense and myrrh
    But know not of their significance
    Or their sacrifice
    You seek with my words to hang
    An albatross around your very own necks
    And my own!
    Amen, I say to you
    My message was not made for such a medium."

"But, Sage!"
    Interrupted another from the crowd
    Whose face I could not see
    "Gone are the days when tasks were domesticated

I now travel a great distance every day
 From my home to my task
 And need something to fill the air
 What message was not made for this medium?"
 At this, the crowd murmured its approval
 In contrast to the beady-eyed villager
 Who I had seen a moment ago
 Upon hearing this
 He sneered and spat on the ground in disgust

Replied the Sage
 "It is not lost upon me that the road is winding
 And the days are long for many
 Far too many of us
 But hear me true!
 Though the pursuit of wisdom is a noble path
 We on this journey must know
 That it will never dwell
 In an auction house

Amen, I say to you
 Beware of the sophists and charlatans
 The merchants and technologists
 Who see this void in our lives
 And cater to it for their own ends

Dear friends, knowledge is a jewel
 But it can neither be bought nor sold
 Knowledge is wrought from diligence
 But it is a diligence nurtured organically

Far from inanimate machinations and acrylic light
    Those who seek to tell you otherwise
    Will only lead you astray

Hark, the acrylic audio you consume
    On the path to daily tasks
    The colorful, pixelated madness
    Which fills your days and nights
    Are offered by sophists and charlatans
    Whose agenda deviates from the right and true
    And are buttressed by merchants and technologists
    Seeking to make your knowledge a commodity
    Hear me true!
    Real knowledge is inalienable
    And does not come in a box

Listen and you will hear
    Open your eyes and you will see
    That their interest lies not in enriching you
    But in enriching themselves
    Not in promulgating truth
    But in propagating that which entices you
    Begs you to watch and listen just a moment longer
    You, who pay for neither audio nor pixel
    Must know that you are the product being sold!

Amen, I say to you
    Every time such beings open their mouths

They prove their discontent
    Listen to the Sages of yore who wisely said
    It is better to remain silent and be thought a fool
    Than to speak out and remove all doubt."

Shuffling the box of Amazin' gift cards
    The Sage declared
    "Before you think me a hypocrite
    Hear me this
    These cards, which beckoned you to me
    Were not provided from on high
    I have not come from a gilded wedding
    Atop a floating city
    But rather from among you
    Yea, I purchased these cards with my own funds
    In the hopes that some of you would hear me true
    And that a tremendous event
    Would spill forth from among us
    Through these worn cobblestone streets
    And along the cracks in the sidewalk."

Hearing all this, the young woman retreated back
    Sheepishly again into the crowd of people
    Thus spoke the Sage
    "Fame is not what I seek
    For fame neither precedes nor succeeds truth
    Dear friends, while all the world may be a stage
    We cannot all be players
    And though there remains a great task before us all
    There is nobility in seclusion
    Indeed the heroes among us work in silence

In the shadows cast by acrylic light and neon gods
    Rather than in their false lights

Amen, I say to you
    Peace and freedom shall be found in the ordinary
    Rather than the extraordinary."

11

A SONG OF CITIZENRY

At this juncture
 The police became more agitated
 Their badges bristling in the breeze
 As their unhindered hands shifted to their holsters
 Slowly and gradually
 As if by happenstance
 As if the world were not
 In cosmic movement atop their shoulders

Just then, the beady-eyed villager
 Whose marble eyes glistened with rage
 Undeterred by the hesitation of the police
 For whom he had long been an earworm
 Further angered by the Sage's continued presence
 Raised his raspy voice and declared
 "Will no one stop this scoundrel?
 I have heard him whine long enough!
 I have lived here my whole life
 And have never seen him before

Who is he to say he is one of us?
  Who is he to speak to us
  With such condescension for our way of life?
  Does he not know
  That we have always done things this way?
  He who speaks so much of the swamp
  Should return to it
  Light to light
  Dust to dust
  And mud to mud for him!"

With this, the crowd began to grumble
  Their faces lifted from the gift cards
  And turned to each other
  As if wondering what to do
  The Sage's voice
  Laden with reason and calling the crowd forward
  Had been replaced with angry cries
  Calling the crowd backward
  To the musty, familiar smell of yesteryear
  To the innate mistrust which always
  Seems to manifest when greeted by
  Something new and different
  Unfazed even still, the Sage spoke unto them again
  This time with a grin

"Perhaps it is true
  That this soil may be fertile after all!
  Just as the great and mighty oak towers over you now
  So did it begin as a small acorn
  Lying inconspicuously on the ground

Before sprouting forth in grandeur
    Perhaps, too, my message
    Long forgotten and unknown on this street corner
    Has finally taken root
    Take heart, my dear friends
    And know that changing the world
    Or any of its parts
    Must come to pass only with ruffled feathers."

But, at this, the beady-eyed man interrupted
    "How can you say you are changing the world
    You feckless old fool?
    You are doing nothing but blocking this street corner
    Distracting these people from their daily tasks
    Which are far more important than yours!"

Spoke the Sage in response
    "My task is the task of all the people
    For the onus is on all of us
    Yourself included
    To identify the shortcomings of society
    The twisted and forgotten corners of civilization
    And develop solutions that solve them
    Amen, I say to you
    The moral arc of the universe bends in no direction
    But in the one which we, ourselves, fashion for it
    With dry, speckled hands

We are fortunate to live in this village
    An oasis of humanity

Amidst the scourge of the wild
    Imperfect though it may be
    It is infinitely better than
    The one from which we came
    Even more grateful we should be
    For the fact that it is malleable
    And temperate
    Amen, I say to you
    Our democratic republic is a crown jewel
    A family heirloom forged and passed down
    Across generations
    Yet whose value is determined
    By those who have taken it for granted
    Beauty is, after all,
    In the eye of the beholder
    Rather than the betrothed

My dear friends, hear me true!
    This crown jewel is never more than one oversight
    One careless gesture
    Away from destruction
    Yes, indeed
    One wrong step can lead us all
    Down the road to perdition
    Although her edges appear strong enough
    To withstand the abrasion of a sandstorm
    Or a fall from a great height
    Surely you can see
    That time has made these edges grow soft
    Do you not see the glee of your enemies
    With their toothless grins
    Reflecting amid her fault lines?

I can hear them licking their chops
    Salivating at the sight of you
    As you squabble among yourselves
    Obsessing over teenage acne
    On a young village's face
    Can you hear it, too?

Dwell not on such trivial matters
    When there are far more important issues at hand
    But do not become complacent in yourselves
    Or in the gradual progression of this village
    Out of the swamp
    Do not let the affairs of the village
    Catch you sleeping soundly and blithely
    Do not conclude this experiment a success
    While it remains in its trial
    For it is clear to see that we are not
    So far removed from the creatures in the swamp

Dear friends,
    Fortune is like a stallion
    Running through the meadows
    Nonplussed by the weight of freedom
    Interested only in the sum total
    Of the blades of grass which pass it by
    Ignorant of the prodding of its hooves
    Along the seldom trodden roads
    Coursing through corners of your minds
    The stallion has no rider
    Has no master
    And knows not where it goes

Amen, I say to you
>Do not lend to fortune
>Any more than you would be willing to lose
>Don your spurs, throw a saddle on the stallion
>Guide it with the reins
>Fashioned by the Sages of before
>Handed to you with bloodied and shaking hands
>Hear me true
>If you fail to break the stallion
>It will buck you and throw you under it
>Whereupon you will be trampled
>And left bruised and broken
>Upon the very ground you were meant to romp

While it is true that fortune favors
>Those bold enough to sit in the saddle
>This, alone, does not make a horseman
>Horsemanship requires more than bravery
>More than audacity
>Amen, I say to you
>Horsemanship requires a careful balance
>Of reins and spurs
>And vision to lead the stallion forward
>Ever forward to the horizon
>Using reins to ensure that, all the while,
>It neither fatigues from overwork
>Nor atrophies from underwork
>And using spurs in a manner
>Which steadfastly propels it forward
>Without drawing blood
>Or inciting rebellion

My dear friends
    Only in this majestic ride through the meadow
    As the sun sets against the distant rolling hills
    We can hear sounding
    The clarion call of citizenry

You must make like a horseman
    And lead this village
    Be active in promoting community
    Be vocal in service of the right and just
    Be relentless in your pursuit
    Of that which will improve it
    For yourself, for others, and for progeny
    For it is that no one but you
    And you, and you, and you
    Can maintain the bearings of this village
    Amen, I say to you
    The burden is on us and us alone
    To keep the compasses pointing north
    To keep the sand in the hourglass
    To keep the sky and earth separated by the horizon
    We must all do our bit
    So that the magnets do not lose their force
    So that axles continue to suspend us over the abyss
    So that we do not one day find ourselves
    Lost and uncoordinated
    Meandering dispassionately
    Through the very realm of our forefathers' passions!
    Be not blind to the creatures without and within
    Who seek to do harm via malevolence and apathy
    Amen, I say to you
    This village and its democratic norms

Are not owned but rather held by you
    For the next generation
    My dear friends
    You must cherish it accordingly
    And protect it always

But hear me true
    Just as you must be courageous in pursuit of all this
    So is it just as important
    That you remain wise and alert
    Toward that which is out of your control
    Or not in the interest of the village
    And let it peacefully and soundly pass you by
    For dwelling on it extensively
    Will only tear your soul asunder
    And wreak havoc on your mind and bones
    Remember, dear friends,
    That when you are presented with such stressors
    And you will be!
    View them not as problems requiring solutions
    But rather as wrinkles in the universe
    Bridging a space and time
    Which are already connected
    By the sinews of temporality
    Be not crumpled by the wrinkles of existence
    And keep your eyes always on your own agency

But make no mistake, dear friends
    And do not forget what I have spoken earlier
    Stallions, like human beings
    Like cosmic wrinkles

Like all things that exist on this earth
    And perhaps beyond
    Will come and go in youthful splendor
    Shine brightly for a brief, glorious moment
    Before fading ever softly
    Graying most gradually
    Slowing down and hunching over
    Before passing into that which is yet to come

Amen, I say to you
    This village will neither know the face of the sun
    In ten thousand years' time
    Nor the belly of the beast
    From ten thousand years before
    But fear not this interplay of cosmic continuum
    Fear not our minute space herein
    Do not position yourself opposite nature
    By resisting the rising and falling of empires
    For that which sits atop the world
    Has nowhere to go but down
    And hear me true
    It will come crashing down
    Like a sine curve!
    So it was in the beginning
    So it is now and ever shall be
    One world with shifting ends

Amen, I say to you
    Be fervent in your rise
    And dignified in your fall

Take heart in the glory of now
    Take pride in the power bestowed upon you
    And all the village this day

The power to breathe air
    And expel it into the current moment
    What a blessing this is!
    Do this and you will see that there is no greater gift
    Lest such a noble procession pass us by,
    Do this, and you will see that it truly becomes so
    A timeless interpretation of our timed reality
    Amen, I say to you
    This precious mystery
    An ongoing experiment within the state of nature
    A rolling stone en route to the depths of the sea
    A constant progression toward a more perfect union
    While we may never reach our intended destination
    Let this not be an excuse for failing to step forward
    Let this cause us to sweat
    So that we may feel the salt
    As we wipe it from our faces

My dear friends
    Despite the animosity
    The inefficiency
    The sweating and the pain
    Never forget to see the beauty
    In the nobility of the work completed before us
    Or the magnificence of the work which is yet to come
    Let this neither perish from the earth
    Nor slip the bonds of your mind."

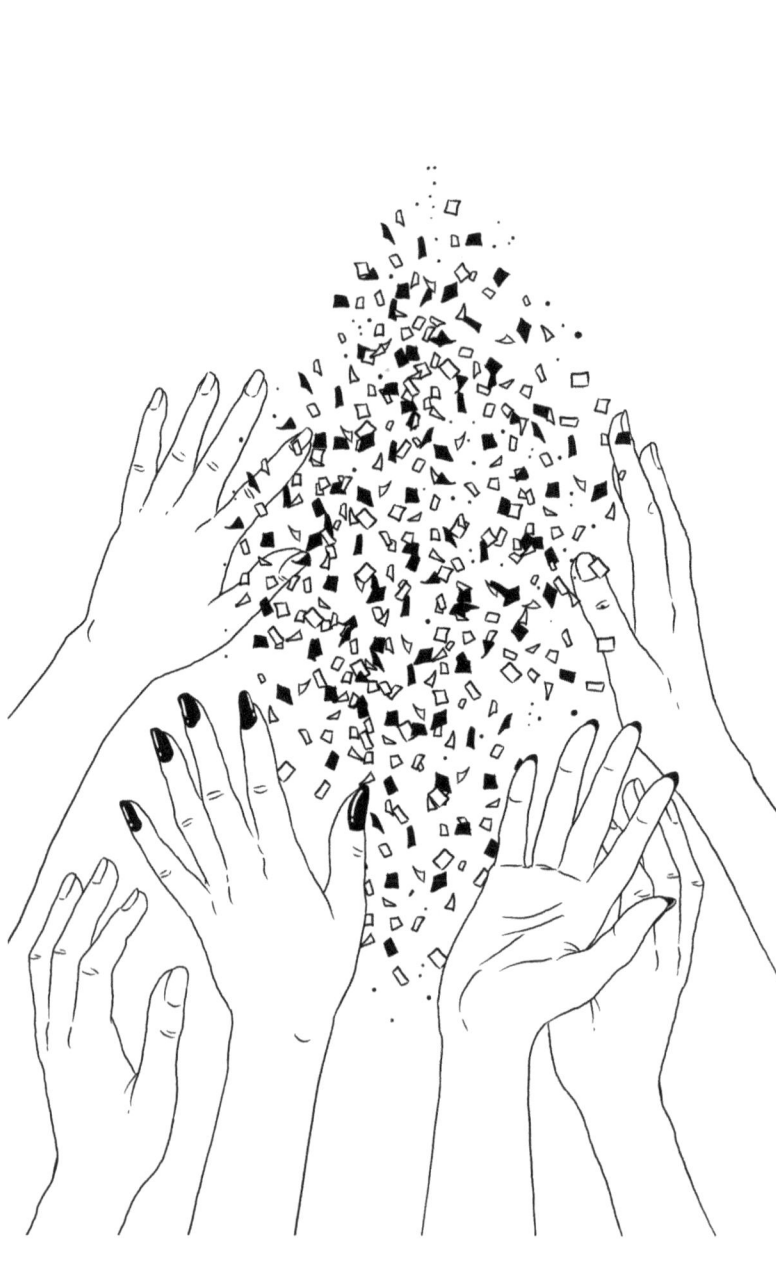

12

A BRIDGE AND CHORUS

When the Sage finished speaking
    And likely at the direction of the beady-eyed villager
    The police began forcing
    Began pushing their way through the crowd
    Toward that street corner
    From which had sprouted
    All this controversy

Spoke the Sage
    "But officers, please
    Won't you tell me what this is about?
    In what way have I offended you
    Or this village?
    In fact, I have done nothing
    But extol its virtues
    And seek to improve
    Where it otherwise lacks."

Upon reaching the street corner
    One officer responded
    "Do you have a license to sell these gift cards?
    If you do not
    Then you are in violation of our laws
    And will need to be punished."

With eyes made gloomy and dim
    By the light refracted by the badges approaching
    Spoke the Sage
    "You think of these gift cards
    And not of what I have spoken
    Your bodies are drowning in isolation
    And your minds consist of acrylic paste
    As you remain occupied by two-day free shipping
    And not on what will happen after
    Does the sponge still retain the ink of our horizon?
    Can you still hear the splitting of the earth
    Exposing what lies beneath these soundless
    Squalid streets?
    Has there been a tremendous event after all?

No, brethren, you misunderstand me
    I seek neither to sell nor to profit!
    My goals do not constitute a sum
    They cannot be counted in ones and zeros
    But rather in stones and leaves
    And folly be to you
    For I have not purchased these gift cards
    For resale or for wholesale
    But rather for gifting and regifting

So that some truth may be gleaned
    From the revolutions of the earth
    Surely you know it is better to give than to receive!"

"Anger yourself not with me,"
    Spoke the officer
    As he and the others surrounded the street corner
    Encircling the Sage
    "There is a shopkeeper in the crowd
    Who operates in accordance with our laws
    And he has suggested to us
    That you are infringing on his business
    In an unlawful manner
    And we, as you mentioned,
    Are just doing our jobs."

I then noticed the beady-eyed villager
    Beaming brightly
    His grin nearly splitting his face in two
    Making clear to all within view
    The chunks of his breakfast
    Between his teeth

Spoke the Sage
    With a twinkle in his eye
    And a devilish grin on his face
    "Hear me, you who expect me to produce a license
    To speak the truth
    You who come here under the false pretense
    Of clamping down on the black market

While commenting not on Autovana
  And DividedHealthcare
  Your motive is plain as day!
  Lay down the keys to your tabernacle
  For you do not need a chalice
  To kiss the sea and drink up its waters

Amen, I say to you
  Go forth to smell the seabed
  And dance with the crabs
  While I return to the mountaintop
  Far beyond the hallowed swamp
  From there, I can soak up the sun
  As I view all the land
  Upon which it reflects
  There I will wait until it is safe
  For me to return to this village
  Or to any of the others
  Which came before you
  Or are destined to come after

There I will hope and pray
  That your hearts of flesh
  Will not have converted to stone
  Begging to be carved by the sharpest chisel
  Amen I say to you
  You have been provided the ink and quill
  But your history remains to be written
  You can hear the sounds of the earth

But must slow the beating of your heart to do so
    In my words
    Or in the songs of your own souls
    You may speak the truth
    Only after you stop acting like fish
    Cursing the bubbles that form
    From your huffing and puffing
    Rebelling against the current
    Wondering what water is."

I swear to you
    The Sage fixed his gaze upon me
    It appeared as though he could see right through me
    As he said
    "I depart you now
    Go forth in love and power."

Thus the Sage picked up the box of gift cards
    And retreating softly
    Into the warm caress of the cracked sidewalk
    Down the road from the street corner
    Along a path hitherto untraveled
    By shoes so torn and worn
    By the authority borne by existence
    Threw the box into the air
    Allowing the cards to scatter
    Like snowflakes on a winter morning
    Like the dewfall on the cusp of dawn
    And swiftly disappeared into the crowd

Which swarmed the falling gift cards
    Like children rushing toward a Christmas tree
    Like wolves descending upon a henhouse
    Like a movable matrimony
    Of the concrete and the discrete

13

A SONG FOR THE EVERLASTING

The police were hampered by these masses
    Pounding upon the street corner
    In a rising of uncertain tides
    And some lined their pockets with gift cards
    Which rained down like brimstone
    As they resumed their push
    Through the pulsing multitude
    The beady-eyed shopkeeper
    Grew a vein in his forehead
    Which snaked from his balding head
    To his snarling lips
    And he cursed the Sage
    In a voice which, though I could not hear it
    Surely echoed like tinsel and cellophane
    Crinkling in a distant corner of the world

The police could not locate the Sage
    This much was plainly clear

They scratched their heads
    Strained their necks
    Searching under every nook and cranny
    Every gully and every crack in the sidewalk
    Poring through the rambunctious
    And effervescent crowd
    Like a streamer floating through a mosh pit
    Forever riding the thrill
    Before finding its penultimate sleep
    Blissful rest
    Upon the base of this concrete jungle
    Alas, to no avail!

But where has the Sage gone?
    Inquiring minds would like to know
    Whither do his steps lead
    After immersing himself into the crowd
    Which he so carefully wrought
    With the glittery allure
    Of timeless wisdom and two-day free shipping

Hark! Such a good thing
    Could not truly last long
    In a village of such great potential
    And dripping mud
    Far away from this village, no doubt
    Went the Sage
    To a distant mountaintop, perhaps
    Of which he so fondly spoke
    To soak up the sun

But I confess to you
    That I know neither where the mountain is
    Nor when the Sage will return
    To this swamp, this village
    As was foretold

With great despair, I saw
    The masses slowly return to a previous form
    A swift unwinding of themselves
    As they slinked back aimlessly
    Eyes wandering toward the cracks in the sidewalks
    In blissful ignorance of the rancor
    Of the police searching for the Sage
    Stooping down once again in anger
    As if the world were but a rock in their shoes
    Waiting to be removed by cold, unfeeling fingers

How could it be that the Sage's words
    Could be so quickly forgotten?
    I thought to myself
    How quickly the minds of mortals
    Forget that which is truly important
    After something shiny crosses their surly minds?
    How difficult it is to change reality
    Once comfort has been found in the discomfort?
    What a feat of impermanence this is
    For they find pride in their objects
    But cannot see such suffering thereby
    They see wisdom presented to them, face to face
    But forget its contours in the blink of an eye

They seek sufficiency in insufficiency
    As if trying to draw blood from a stone

But just then I saw before me
    A vision I had not seen before
    In this village which
    Had heretofore only presented itself
    As a bastion of the fickle and forgetful
    Of the acrylic and analogue
    I saw a young man and young woman
    Yes, the young man and young woman of before!
    Move their eyes from the street corner
    Toward each other
    I saw a smile part their pursed lips
    As they turned to face each other
    Laughing in symphonic harmony for a few moments
    As the commotion around them
    Formed in unison with the music of their laughter
    Before they connected with a passionate kiss

As the world blurred around them
    In consummation of their simple act of devout love
    As if no one else were truly there
    This, too, sounded like music
    As it echoed in happy ripples
    Across the concrete separating them from the earth
    Separating this union only spatially

As their lips gave way to smiles directed at one another
    They grasped hands and began to swing them

Like children along a seashore
    In sheer joy
    Letting "DividedHealthcare" business cards
    And acrylic panes dotted with acrylic audio
    Fall in splendor
    Like soft rains to the cobblestones
    Upon which they meandered
    With eyes forward
    To the sky

I will ask myself no more
    What am I going to be?
    For I can tell you truly
    This is what I am going to be
    And this is how it will be!

Amen, I say to you
    Yes, amen I say to you!
    It matters not where the distant mountaintop is
    It matters not when the Sage will return
    For now, no one can deny
    That the song which began down by the Piraeus
    Though it seems like only yesterday
    Is still being sung today
    And at least one other can hear its tone
    Progress is not inevitable
    But with enough effort it will take root
    And sprout forth from the soil
    Perhaps in this generation or in the next
    In whoever is willing to bend ears to hear it

I have heard the music
 Just as you all have
 Perhaps this village is not so cracked
 That it is beyond the salvage of grout
 Laid down tirelessly and ceaselessly
 By the hands of the true and brave

Let rest our cracked and bleeding hands
 For herein lies the salt of this earth
 Let it see our bright and shining faces
 As we greet it with a smile
 Let us hear the song of the earth
 And hum a supporting melody
 Let us feel the wind on our backs
 As we beat onward toward the horizon
 Let the wings we made for ourselves
 Spread as we soar upwards
 To rest among the clouds for only a moment
 Before returning gracefully
 To this blessed ground

Yea, let us sing the song of our nature
 And allow it to slide ourselves
 Our destinies
 In sacrosanct union
 Toward the bright and beautiful world
 That we are capable of willing into our own

Let it be so!

ACKNOWLEDGMENTS

This work would not have been possible without the great thinkers who have left an indelible mark on the tapestry of humanity, without those who introduced me to them, and without the ceaseless support of all those who have shown me unconditional love.

ABOUT THE AUTHOR

Zachary D. Lynch grew up in New England but has called Florida home since 2020. As a practicing attorney, he addresses tangible issues that affect his clients in the course of their daily lives. As a lifelong student of philosophy and prose, however, he retains an awareness of certain intangible issues that affect all people in the course of their entire lives. Reconciling these is a difficult endeavor, but one that piques his interest.